THE DEVIL'S ARITHMETIC

by
Jane Yolen

Teacher Guide

Written by
Elizabeth M. Klar
and Cheryl Klar-Trim

Edited by
Katherine E. Martinez

Note

The Puffin paperback edition of this book, published by Viking Penguin Inc., ©1988, was used to prepare this guide. Page references may differ in other editions.

Please note: Parts of this novel deal with sensitive, mature issues. Please assess the appropriateness of this book for the age level and maturity of your students prior to reading and discussing it with your class.

ISBN 1-58130-684-9

To order, contact your local school supply store, or—

Novel Units, Inc.
P.O. Box 433
Bulverde, TX 78163-0433

Web site: www.educyberstor.com

Table of Contents

Skills and Strategies

Thinking
Research, compare/contrast, pros/cons, brainstorming, problem solving, creative thinking, identifying stereotypes, critical thinking

Listening/Speaking
Dramatizing, interviewing, story-telling, discussion, oral reports, recording, music

Vocabulary
Target word charades, target word maps, synonyms, antonyms, defining, root/base words, context clues

Literary Elements
Literary analysis, story mapping, characterization, foreshadowing

Comprehension
Predicting, sequencing, inference, cause/effect

Writing
Character journal, memories, personal writing, creative writing, headlines, poetry

Across the Curriculum
Social studies–geography; Health–nutrition; Art–drawing, advertisements, collage

Summary

The Devil's Arithmetic tells the story of Hannah, a young girl who is transported back to pre-Nazi Poland. She experiences many hardships while at the camp. Hannah also learns valuable life lessons. She learns to be a giver instead of a taker, and she learns that one must remember the past in order to help those who will come in the future. Hannah also comes to realize that the Holocaust must never be forgotten.

About the Author

Jane Yolen comes from an American Jewish family whose Yolen grandparents came over in the early 1900s. Her Berlin, Germany, grandparents settled in Virginia about the same time. Her daughter's Hebrew name is Chaya, which means "life." *The Devil's Arithmetic* is a National Jewish Book Award winner and an American Bookseller "Pick of the Lists."

Introductory Activities

1. Previewing the book: Have students look at the cover and answer the journalist's questions about what they see: Who? When? Where? What? and Why? Based on their answers, students predict what the book will be about.

2. Predicting: Given the following clues, students write a paragraph predicting what they think will happen in the story.

   time-travel   heroism   sacrifice   evil   concentration camp

3. Character Journal: List the main characters from *The Devil's Arithmetic* and have students choose one. As they read the book, students write regular entries from that character's point of view. Journal entries should reflect on the events of the story. At various points in their reading, have students share their journals with classmates.

4. Attribute Web: Create an attribute web (see page 10 of this guide) with students for each of the following ideas: friends, the Holocaust, bravery, love, and memories. Ask students to quickly tell what each word brings to mind. Encourage students to elaborate on particular ideas.

5. Prediction Chart: Have students set up a prediction chart (see pages 6-7 of this guide) to use as they read the book.

6. Anticipation Questions: Have students respond to each of the following statements with a "thumbs up" (I agree) or a "thumbs down" (I disagree) and discuss their responses.
   - Stories about the past are always boring.
   - It is better to be a giver than a taker.
   - Friends should help and support each other.
   - It is important to protect children.
   - Love is shown in different ways.
   - We can help the future generations by learning from mistakes of the past.

Vocabulary Activities

1. Target Word Charades: Have students act out some of the vocabulary words and have classmates guess the target word. Some suggested words for *The Devil's Arithmetic*:

swoop (7)	jostling (51)	protruding (73)	stench (78)
rummaged (98)	contorted (123)	thudding (147)	

2. Target Word Maps: Have students complete word maps for vocabulary words of a certain part of speech. For example, adjectives from *The Devil's Arithmetic* would include:

unleavened (5)	elaborate (30)	companionable (35)	appreciative (51)
barbed (150)	ironic (168)	indelible (169)	

```
┌──────────────┐                      ┌──────────────┐
│   Synonym    │                      │   Antonym    │
└──────────────┘                      └──────────────┘
              ┌──────────────┐
              │    WORD      │
              └──────────────┘
┌──────────────┐                      ┌──────────────┐
│  Define in   │                      │  Use in a    │
│your own words│                      │  sentence    │
└──────────────┘                      └──────────────┘
```

3. Sentences: Have students select five or six vocabulary words and use as many of the words as possible in one sentence.

4. Synonym Match: Have students select vocabulary words from a chapter and list one synonym for each vocabulary word on a small piece of paper. Students mix the pieces of paper and match each synonym to the appropriate vocabulary word.

5. Root/Base Words: Have students find the base or root word for at least eight vocabulary words. Students look at each word and answer the following questions: What is the meaning of the root word? What is the meaning of the vocabulary word? What prefix or suffix has been added to the vocabulary word? What is the meaning of the prefix or suffix? How has the meaning of the root/base word changed by adding the prefix or suffix?

6. Vocabulary Sort: Have the students sort vocabulary words into categories (e.g., nouns, verbs, and adjectives/adverbs).

7. Odd One Out: Use vocabulary words from one or two chapters. Have the students make a chain of four words. One word in the chain is the vocabulary word, two words are synonyms for the vocabulary word, and one word does not go with the others. (Mix the sequence of the words in the chain.) Students should exchange their chains and underline the word that does not belong with the others and explain why it does not belong.

8. Vocabulary Boxes: Cut a pattern for a cube (pattern included) from construction paper. Before the cube is glued together, each face should contain one of the following: a vocabulary word, the definition of the word, illustration of the word, a synonym of the word, antonym of the word, a sentence using the word. Display the vocabulary boxes in the room.

9. Star Match: Have students cut large golden stars or another shape from construction paper. The students should write a vocabulary word on one side of the star and its definition on the other side. Glue a piece of Velcro on the word side of the star. Attach the star to a bulletin board that has been covered with felt. Teams or individual students will choose a star (definitions are written on the front side). If the student can say the vocabulary word that matches the definition, he/she may keep the star. The team or individual who has the most stars wins the game.

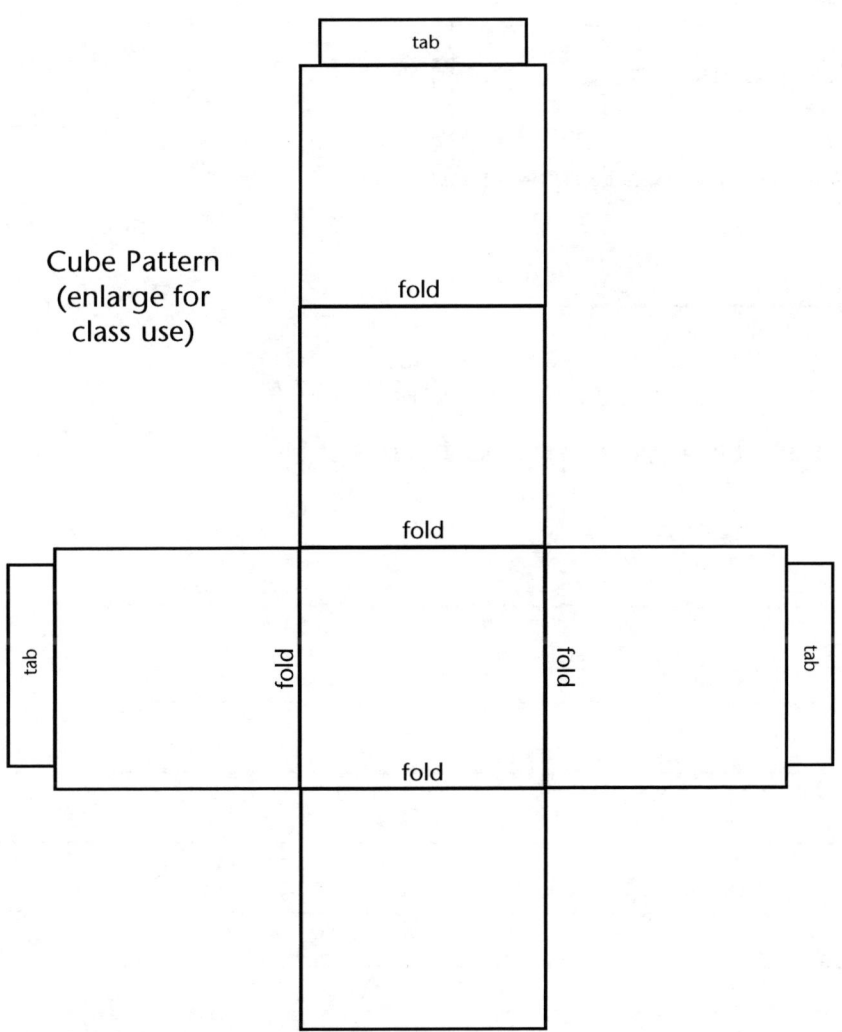

Cube Pattern
(enlarge for
class use)

Using Predictions in the Novel Unit Approach

We all make predictions as we read—little guesses about what will happen next, how a conflict will be resolved, which details will be important to the plot, which details will help fill in our sense of a character. Students should be encouraged to predict, to make sensible guesses as they read the novel.

As students work on their predictions, these discussion questions can be used to guide them: What are some of the ways to predict? What is the process of a sophisticated reader's thinking and predicting? What clues does an author give to help us make predictions? Why are some predictions more likely to be accurate than others?

Create a chart for recording predictions. This could be either an individual or class activity. As each subsequent chapter is discussed, students can review and correct their previous predictions about plot and characters as necessary.

Use the facts and ideas the author gives.

Use your own prior knowledge.

Apply any new information (i.e., from class discussion) that may cause you to change your mind.

Predictions:

_____

_____

_____

_____

Prediction Chart

What characters have we met so far?	What is the conflict in the story?	What are your predictions?	Why did you make those predictions?

Using Character Webs in the Novel Unit Approach

Attribute webs are simply a visual representation of a character from the novel. They provide a systematic way for students to organize and recap the information they have about a particular character. Attribute webs may be used after reading the novel to recapitulate information about a particular character, or completed gradually as information unfolds. They may be completed individually or as a group project.

One type of character attribute web uses these divisions:

- How a character acts and feels. (How does the character act? How do you think the character feels? How would you feel if this happened to you?)

- How a character looks. (Close your eyes and picture the character. Describe him/her to me.)

- Where a character lives. (Where and when does the character live?)

- How others feel about the character. (How does another specific character feel about our character?)

In group discussion about the characters described in student attribute webs, the teacher can ask for backup proof from the novel. Inferential thinking can be included in the discussion.

Attribute webs need not be confined to characters. They may also be used to organize information about a concept, object, or place.

Attribute Web

The attribute web below will help you gather clues the author provides about a character in the novel. Fill in the blanks with words and phrases which tell how the character acts and looks, as well as what the character says and what others say about him or her.

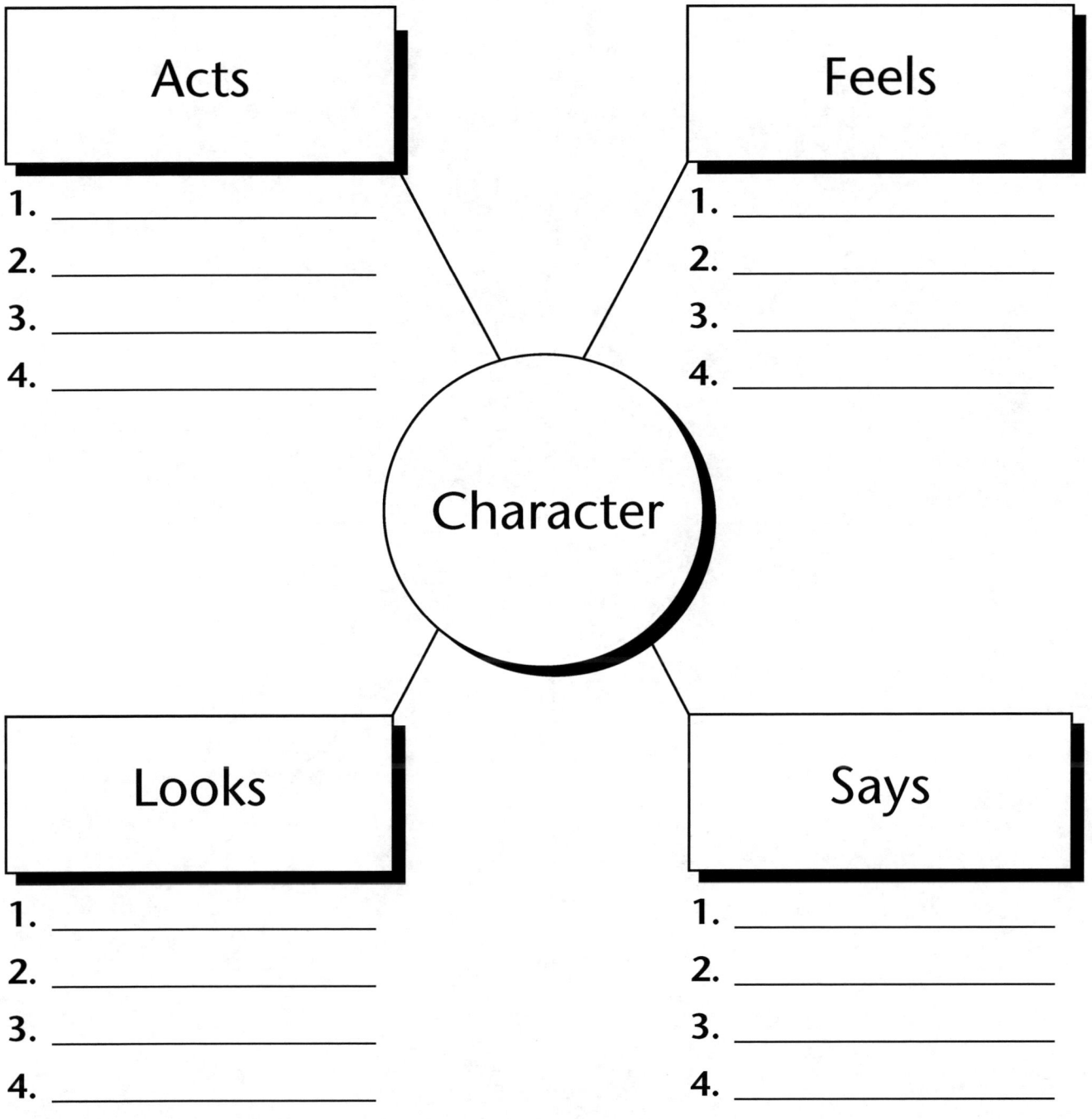

9

Attribute Web

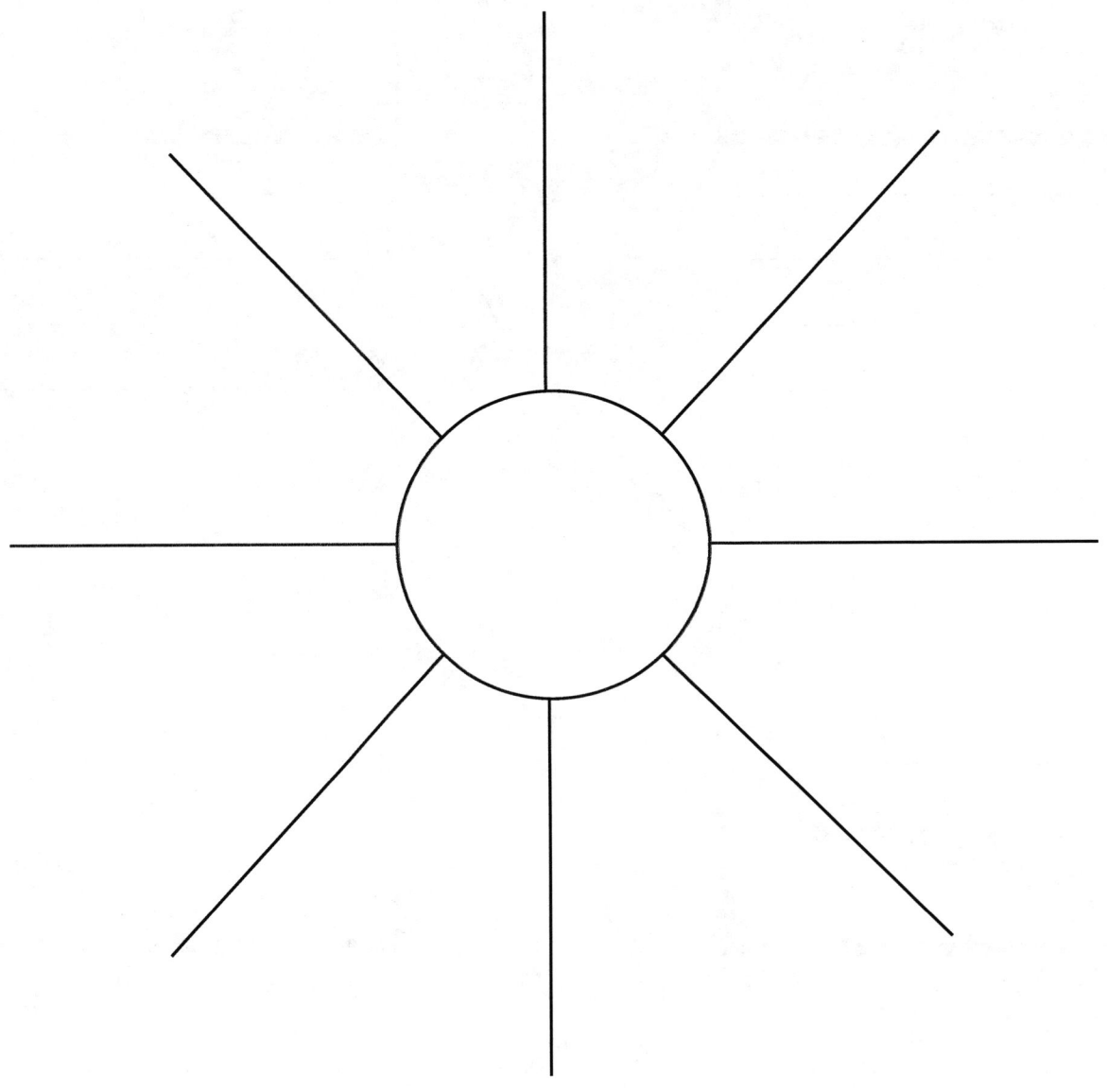

Story Map

Directions: Record the setting, characters, and problem first. Then follow the arrow to the plot line to record the increasing conflict and incidents leading to the climax. Note the turning point and resolution.

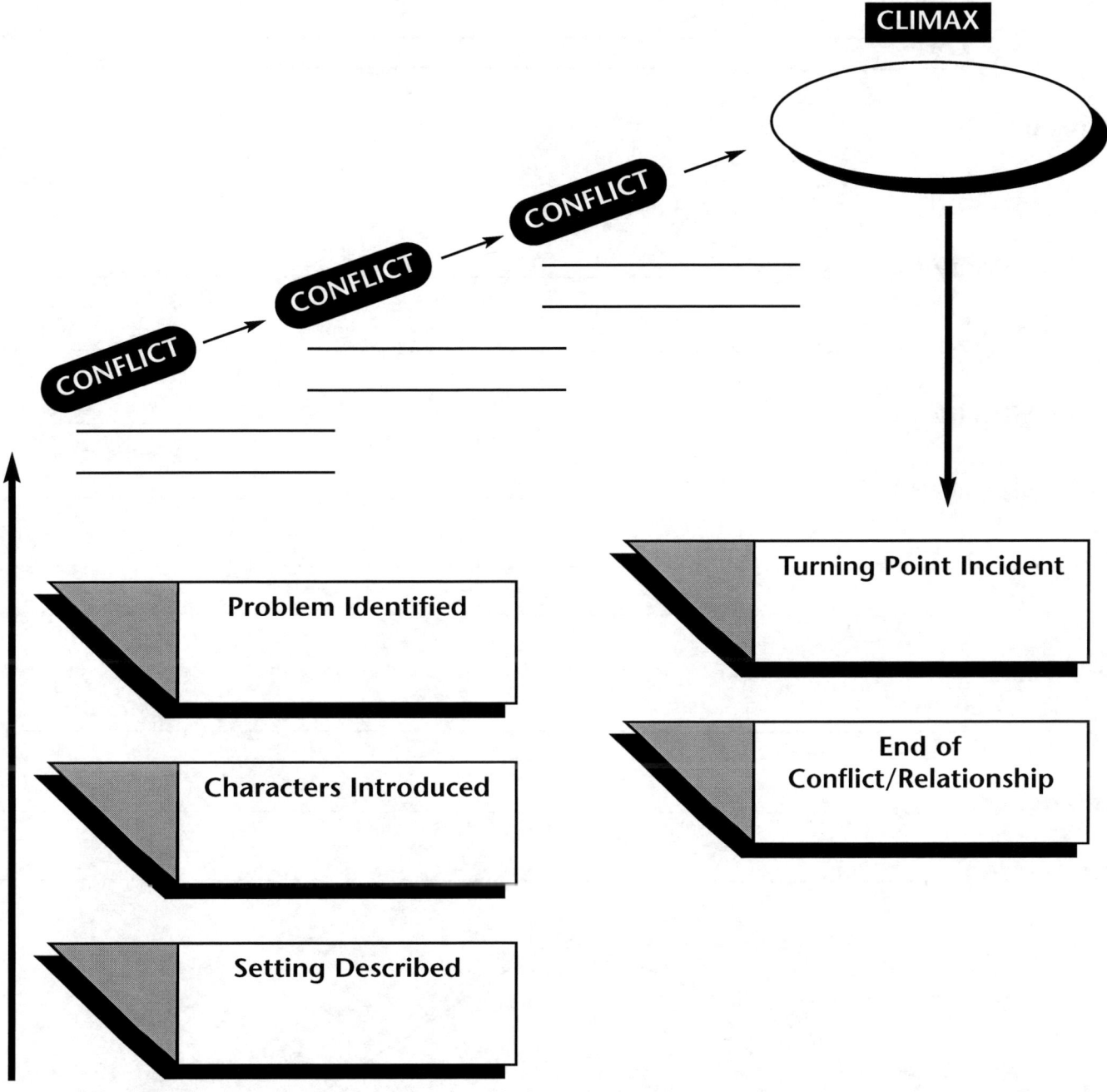

Story Map

Title: _____

Setting:
┌───┐
│   │
│   │
└───┘

Problem:
┌───┐
│   │
│   │
└───┘

Difficulty #1 _____

Difficulty #2 _____

Difficulty #3 _____

Difficulty #4 _____

Climax (Difficulty) _____

Resolution:
┌───┐
│   │
│   │
└───┘

Protagonist: _____

Antagonist: _____

Protagonist

Climax

Conflict

Resolution

Chapters 1-2

Vocabulary

flushed (3)	Passover (3)	Seder (3)	Yiddish (4)
unleavened (5)	Haggadah (5)	pounced (6)	gruesome (6)
swoop (7)	dreading (7)	concentration camp (8)	cordwood (8)
uncomprehendingly (9)	distorted (9)	guttural (9)	steerage (10)
saga (10)	compensation (10)	preferred (10)	frustration (12)

Discussion Questions

1. Why does Hannah's mother keep smiling and talking in a low voice as she argues with Hannah? *(She doesn't want anyone at Rosemary's house to know that she and Hannah are arguing.)*

2. Why doesn't Hannah want to go to the Seder? *(She and Aaron will be the only children there and the punch lines to all the jokes will be in Yiddish.)*

3. What does Hannah seem to think Passover is about? What does Hannah's mother say that Passover is really about? *(eating; remembering)*

4. Why is having their entire family present on Passover so important to Grandpa Will and Grandma Belle? *(The Nazis killed most of their family members during WWII.)*

5. Why is Hannah's patience with Aaron wearing thin? *(He can't remember the Four Questions.)*

6. What does Hannah say she will do if Aaron can't remember the Four Questions? *(She will whisper them in his ear the way they do in plays when someone forgets a line.)*

7. Why is Hannah glad to tell Aaron a story? *(She is glad to be doing something she is good at.)*

8. Why does Hannah decide not to get upset that she didn't get to push the elevator button? *(She remembers how scared she was the first time she had to ask the Four Questions at the Seder, and she doesn't want to upset Aaron.)*

9. Why do you think Aunt Rose believes everyone in her family is the most beautiful, the smartest, and the greatest, even if it isn't true? *(Answers will vary.)*

10. Why does Hannah feel guilty about washing off Aunt Eva's kiss? *(Aunt Eva is her favorite aunt and the only one who seems to prefer her to her brother Aaron.)*

11. Why is everyone gathered in a tight semi-circle around Grandpa Will? *(Grandpa Will is watching a TV program about the Holocaust and getting upset.)*

12. Why does Grandpa Will shake his fist at the TV and yell, "Give them this!"? *(He is angry with the Nazis for what happened to him and his family during World War II.)*

13. Why do you think Grandpa Will was angry with Hannah for writing numbers like his on her left arm? *(Answers will vary.)*

14. Why doesn't Grandpa Dan get upset over the war like Grandpa Will? *(Grandpa Dan was never in the concentration camps.)*

15. Why doesn't Hannah want any of her friends to meet Grandpa Will? *(She is afraid he will shout at them or do something crazy.)*

16. Why do you think Aunt Eva never married? *(Answers will vary.)*

Supplementary Activities

1. Research: Have students consult reference books for answers to the following questions: What is the Passover? Where did it originate? When did it originate? List four to six reasons why the Passover is observed now. How are Easter and Passover related?

2. Story Maps: Have students begin a story map (see pages 11-12 of this guide) to use as they read the story. As they read the book, they should continue to add new information about the characters, setting, problems, and events of the story.

3. Character Analysis: Have students begin a character attribute web (see pages 8-10 of this guide) for Hannah.

4. Research/Religion: As a class, research which food items are appropriate for a Seder meal. Assign one food item per child to bring to school, and then share the food.

Chapters 3-4

Vocabulary

droned (13)	exodus (13)	mortified (14)	rousing (15)
cloying (16)	kosher (17)	wisps (17)	throb (19)
fraud (19)	ripely (20)	pelted (20)	smudged (23)
kerchief (23)	illusion (23)	hypnotic (23)	contagious (25)
wry (26)	cascaded (26)	conspiratorial (27)	goosedown (30)

Discussion Questions

1. Why do you think Uncle Will hushes Hannah when she tries to say that they aren't conducting the Seder in the right order? *(Answers will vary.)*

2. How will the Seder at Grandpa Dan's be different from the Seder with Grandpa Will? *(There will be three cousins her own age to play with, she'll get to sit in the kitchen away from the adults, and Grandpa Dan won't shout and make a scene.)*

3. How does Hannah know that Aaron is unhappy as he reads the Second Question? *(His voice gets too loud and he finishes in a rush.)*

4. Why does Hannah blurt out, "It isn't fair!"? *(She is angry at the thought of having to eat bitter herbs while her friend Rosemary gets to eat jellybeans.)*

5. Why does Grandpa Will always get his way when he says things like, "when my sister Eva was thirteen, what she would have given for a little glass of watered wine..."? *(He makes people feel guilty for the horrors he and Eva went through in the concentration camp.)*

6. Why is Aaron so excited when no one finds the hidden *afikoman*? *(He thinks he is clever for hiding it so well and that he will get a prize.)*

7. Why does Hannah offer her whole glass of wine to Elijah? *(She is feeling sick from drinking the wine.)*

8. What does Grandpa Will mean when he says, "A sacrifice unasked is so much the greater"? *(Answers will vary.)*

9. Why does Hannah feel guilty about getting to open the door for Elijah? *(She feels like a fraud being given the honor because she didn't offer her wine as a sacrifice but because she didn't want it.)*

10. What causes Hannah to be transported back in time to Poland? *(Answers will vary.)*

11. What significance does the name "Chaya" have for Hannah? *(It is the Hebrew name given to her to honor Aunt Eva's dead friend.)*

12. Why does Hannah think she is only dreaming and that she is not really Chaya? *(She remembers her family, her friend Rosemary, and her life in New Rochelle.)*

13. What explanation do Shmuel and Gitl have for Chaya's odd behavior? *(They think she is still recovering from her illness and the death of her parents.)*

14. Why do you think Hannah doesn't explain that she is not Chaya? *(Answers will vary.)*

15. Why do you think Gitl doesn't want to marry Yitzchak? Do you think she still loves Avrom? *(She says that Yitzchak is a monster and only wants a nurse for his children. Answers will vary.)*

16. How do you think Hannah feels as Gitl tells her that she and Shmuel are her family now? Do you think Gitl and Shmuel will be kind to Hannah? *(Answers will vary.)*

17. What would you do if you were Hannah? *(Answers will vary.)*

Supplementary Activities

1. Research: During the Seder, Grandpa Will recites stories about the plagues and the exodus from Egypt. Have students research the plagues that occurred before the exodus.

2. Research: Have students research the exodus from Egypt. They should answer the following questions: Who was involved in the exodus? Where did the exodus take place? When did the exodus take place? Why did the exodus take place?

3. Writing: Have the students pretend that they are journalists during the exodus. They are to write a newspaper headline and short article about this event.

4. Prediction: Have the students predict what might happen to Hannah after she finds herself in Shmuel's house (see pages 6-7 of this guide).

5. Compare and Contrast: Have the students compare and contrast the home of Hannah's Grandfather and the home of Shmuel using a Venn diagram.

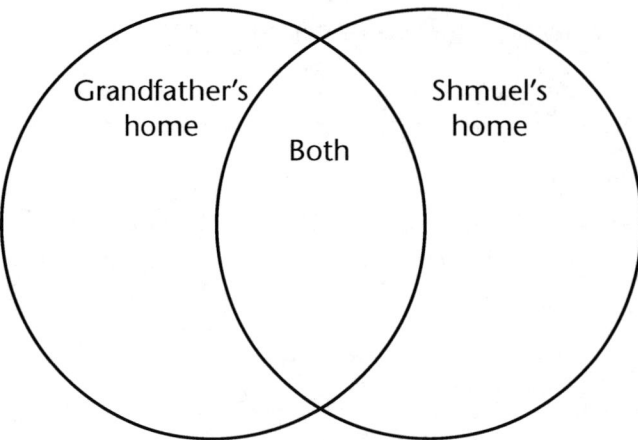

Chapters 5-6

Vocabulary

feathered (33)	tentatively (33)	humoring (34)	companionable (35)
mused (36)	expansively (37)	snick (38)	slovens (39)
henpecked (40)	swipe (40)	smock (41)	distinguish (41)
privy (42)	plaits (43)	timidity (44)	crocks (45)
threaded (45)	goyish (46)	ferrety (47)	appalled (49)

Discussion Questions

1. What does Hannah think will happen when she opens the front door of Gitl and Shmuel's home the first morning she awakens there? *(She will open the door and be back home.)*

2. Why does Hannah remember her family in New Rochelle as part of some dream? *(Answers will vary.)*

3. What does Shmuel mean when he says, "A girl's dreams should be sweet and filled with honey"? *(Answers will vary.)*

4. How does Shmuel react when Hannah tells him she is not Chaya? Why does he react this way? *(He thinks she is confused or that she is playing a game with him. To him, she is Chaya. The Chaya he knows speaks Lublinese Yiddish.)*

5. Why does Hannah shiver as she puts on Chaya's ugly black boots? *(They fit too perfectly, which makes her start to think she may really be Chaya.)*

6. Why is Hannah disappointed by the breakfast Gitl made? *(She was hoping for a big breakfast, but all Gitl offers is milk, coffee, and a loaf of dark bread.)*

7. How is the breakfast food Gitl serves Hannah different from the food she is accustomed to? *(She is used to white bread instead of dark, and homogenized milk instead of milk with cream.)*

8. Why is Hannah suddenly warmed by a small hope after hearing the knock at the door? *(She thinks the knock may be some kind of signal that the dream, the strange play, is over and her family has come to get her.)*

9. Why does Hannah look down at the table as Yitzchak talks to her? *(She is embarrassed by his compliments to her.)*

10. Why does Gitl want to bring Yitzchak's wedding gift with them to Viosk? *(She doesn't want Fayge's family to think that they do not honor their own people with gifts.)*

11. What does Gitl mean when she says Hannah is not a young lady if she knows what a wedding night is? *(She is referring to Hannah's purity and that a proper young lady should not know what happens between a man and a woman on their wedding night.)*

12. Why does Yitzchak come to Shmuel's house early with his children? *(He comes early to help Gitl prepare the house so it will look nice for Fayge.)*

13. What kind of a person do you think Yitzchak is? *(Answers will vary.)*

14. Why do you think that it is getting harder and harder for Hannah to distinguish between what is dream and what is reality? *(Answers will vary.)*

15. Why does Hannah have to borrow clothes from Gitl? *(Chaya's clothes and bedding had to be burned because they carried the disease she and her parents suffered from. Because Chaya has only been with Gitl for two days, there has not been enough time to make anything new.)*

16. What does Hannah think of the dark blue sailor-suit dress Gitl offers to loan her for the wedding? *(She thinks it looks ugly and babyish.)*

17. Is Gitl upset by Hannah's reaction to the dress? Why? *(Answers will vary.)*

18. Why do you think Gitl loans Hannah the blue ribbons she was saving for her own wedding? *(Answers will vary.)*

19. Why does Hannah want to hide in the barn with the chickens as the people gather outside her home? *(She is nervous about all the loud, strange men and the laughing, chattering women.)*

20. Why is Gitl so careful in the way she arranges all the gifts for Shmuel's wedding? *(She wants to make sure all the schnorrers in Viosk know that they honor their own.)*

21. Why do you think the other girls are astonished to learn that Hannah has a best friend named Rosemary? *(Rosemary is a Christian name and they can't believe Hannah would have a Christian friend. Probably because there were few, if any Christians in their community, also Jews and Christians didn't normally associate.)*

22. Why do the girls think Hannah must have been very rich when she lived in Lublin? *(She tells them that she lived in a house with eight rooms and a bathroom inside.)*

23. Why are the girls shocked when Hannah tells them she goes to school? How does Hannah's opinion of school seem to differ from her new friends'? *(In their community only boys are allowed to attend school. Hannah seems to dislike school, but the girls have always wanted the opportunity to go to school to learn.)*

24. Why do you think the girls are intrigued by the story of *Yentl*? *(Answers will vary.)*

25. How does Hannah's life in New Rochelle seem to differ from that of Rachel and her friends? *(Hannah goes to school while girls in Rachel's community do not. Hannah lives in a big house with a bathroom inside. The others do not live in big houses. Hannah shops on the weekends, indicating that her family does not follow Jewish law as closely as the families of her new friends.)*

Supplementary Activities

1. Geography: Have the students locate New Rochelle, New York, and Lublin, Poland, in a world atlas. Estimate the distance between the two cities. Compare the current population of the cities.

2. Art: Have the students draw a picture of what they think Hannah might have looked liked when she put on the dark blue sailor-suit dress.

3. Writing: Have the students pretend to be either Hannah or Shmuel and write a journal entry about their feelings before they start off for the wedding.

4. Critical Thinking: Discuss with the students the difference between Hannah's home life in New Rochelle and her life with Gitl. They are to compare food, dwellings, landscapes, ways of making a living, and family relationships.

Chapters 7-8

Vocabulary

vigor (50)	compression (50)	appreciative (51)	jostling (51)
clique (51)	filtered (52)	muddled (52)	clarinet (53)
abrupt (54)	uproariously (55)	jester (56)	prickle (57)
riveted (57)	involuntary (61)	undecipherable (62)	materialized (62)
lucid (63)	Nazis (64)		

Discussion Questions

1. Why do you think the girls are mesmerized by Hannah's stories? *(Answers will vary.)*

2. How does Hannah's popularity with her new friends differ from that with her friends in New Rochelle? Why do you think this is? *(She seems to be the center of attention with her new friends. In New Rochelle, she only had a few close friends. Answers will vary.)*

3. What does Hannah think of the forest around her as she walks to the wedding? *(She thinks it looks more magical than the forest in the* Wizard of Oz.*)*

4. What causes the mood the girls are in to break as they walk to the wedding? How do their feelings change? *(They hear the music from the* klezmer *and begin to get excited in anticipation of the wedding.)*

5. How is Hannah able to sing to the music when she doesn't know the words to the song? *(It is as if her mouth belongs to Chaya but her head belongs to Hannah and she is able to sing.)*

6. Shifre says that marriages in the country seem to be different than those in Lublin. What does she mean by this? *(Jewish marriages are usually arranged by the* shadchan *[marriage broker]; women marry the men their parents pick, but they don't usually marry for of love.)*

7. Do you think the poem the *badchan* makes up about Hannah fits her? Why? *(Answers will vary.)*

8. What does Hannah think Fayge looks like the first time she sees her sitting on the wagon? *(She thinks Fayge is one of the most beautiful women she has ever seen. She looks like a movie star dressed in white. She has long dark curls, gold rings on her hands and dangling from her ears, a strong nose and a fierce, piercing look on her face.)*

9. Why do you think Fayge gets excited when Hannah tells her that Shmuel is also afraid to get married? *(Answers will vary.)*

10. What kind of person do you think Fayge is? Do you think she will get along with Hannah and Gitl? *(Answers will vary.)*

11. What does Hannah see in town that makes her shudder? Why do you think she reacts this way? *(She sees three black cars and twelve army trucks. Answers will vary.)*

12. Why do you think the *badchan* shouts *Malach ha-mavis* when the soldier gets out of the car? Why does that phrase have special meaning to Hannah? *(Answers will vary. Her grandfather shouted the same phrase at Hannah when she drew numbers on her arm.)*

13. How does Hannah react when she realizes the soldiers are Nazis? *(She tries to warn the others to run away and tells them that the Nazis want to kill all the Jews.)*

14. If you were Hannah what would you have done when you realized the Nazis were waiting for you at the top of the hill? *(Answers will vary.)*

15. Why does Reb Boruch continue to approach the Nazis instead of running away like Hannah wanted him to? *(He doesn't believe he should fear men—only God.)*

Supplementary Activities

1. Drama/Storytelling: As a class, talk about people's fascination with oral tales and the tradition of storytelling. Invite a professional storyteller to class.

2. Creative Writing: Pretend that you are Hannah. Write a letter to your family in New Rochelle and tell them about the wedding and the people you've met.

3. Discussion Question: Have you ever known anyone like the *badchan*? How is the person you know similar/different from the *badchan* in the story?

Chapters 9-10

Vocabulary

conferred (65)	undistinguishable (65)	persuasive (66)	plaintive (66)
adamantly (66)	duration (68)	humanely (69)	billeted (69)
desecrate (69)	barreled (71)	crematoria (72)	periphery (73)
protruding (73)	undercurrent (76)	tremulous (76)	stench (78)
spontaneously (79)	hysteria (80)	alienates (81)	impudent (82)

Discussion Questions

1. Does Hannah believe the explanation the Nazis give for wanting the villagers to get on the truck? Why? *(No; She knows that the Nazis killed the Jews during World War II.)*

2. How do you think Fayge and Shmuel feel when they realize they won't be married in the synagogue? *(Answers will vary.)*

3. Why does Fayge shush Hannah when she starts to talk about the concentration camps and death? *(She is afraid Hannah's words will fly up to heaven and call down the Angel of Death.)*

4. If you were Hannah, what would you say to Fayge and Gitl to make them understand the danger they are in? *(Answers will vary.)*

5. Why does Fayge nervously twist her earlobe? *(She is worried about what happened to her mother and grandmother.)*

6. Do you think the *badchan* believes the promises the Nazi colonel tells the group? Why? *(No. He murmurs, "The snake smiles but it shows no teeth." He continues to make similar comments as the rabbi tells the group the promises the Nazis have made.)*

7. Why does Gitl cover Hannah's mouth to prevent her from speaking? *(She is afraid the soldiers will harm Hannah if she speaks out.)*

8. What does Hannah feel like as she stands packed in the truck with the rest of her family? *(like they are cattle going to slaughter)*

9. Why do you think Gitl changes from singing lullabies to singing a somber song about a kidnapper? *(Answers will vary.)*

10. If you were Hannah, do you think you would be better off knowing or not knowing about the Holocaust and what was to come? Why? *(Answers will vary.)*

11. How do you think the villagers feel when they see others' possessions spread out along the tracks? *(Answers will vary.)*

12. Do you think the soldiers are going to take the villager's jewelry and paper for safekeeping? What do you think they are going to do with them? *(No. They are going to steal the villager's possessions.)*

13. Why do the villagers scream and cry after being locked in the boxcar? *(They are tightly packed into the boxcar, there is no room to move, it is hot, and they are afraid they will suffocate.)*

14. Why do you think none of the Nazis respond to the screams and cries from the villagers to be let out of the boxcar? *(Answers will vary.)*

15. Why does Hannah try to make the rabbi believe she is from the future? *(She knows the horrors that await the villagers in the concentration camps and she wants him to believe her so he will do something to help them escape.)*

16. Why do you think the villagers reacted as they did to the cries for help from the villagers on the train? *(Answers will vary.)*

17. Why does Gitl keep shushing Hannah as she confirms the rumors of horror the villagers begin telling in the boxcar? *(Answers will vary.)*

18. What does Gitl say is the reason Jews joke about death? *(because what you laugh at and make familiar can no longer frighten you)*

19. Why does Gitl object to breaking down the doors and running away as Hannah suggests? *(She does not want to leave her home.)*

Supplementary Activities

1. Discussion Question: Have you ever had something that you valued taken from you? What was it? How did you feel when it was taken away?

2. Writing: In the story, as the villagers pass by in the train they cry out to the peasants for help. Have you ever asked for help but were refused the help you needed? Write about your experience. What was the situation? How did you feel when help was denied? How did you resolve the problem?

3. Compare/Contrast: As a class, compare and contrast the freedom Hannah felt walking through the woods to the wedding to the way she felt trapped in the boxcar with the other villagers.

Chapters 11-12

Vocabulary

wail (84)	embankment (86)	runnels (88)	uninflected (88)
baffled (89)	vehemence (89)	amphitheater (89)	vulnerable (91)
discernible (94)	plait (94)	unadorned (97)	dank (97)
rummaged (98)	crooning (100)	affirmation (101)	barracks (101)
rote (102)	ingrate (102)	ominous (102)	dissipating (102)

Discussion Questions

1. How does Hannah know that the train traveled for four days and nights? *(She can tell by how hot and how cold the train becomes.)*

2. Why are the people grateful that they are all in close quarters at night? *(It is very cold at night and they keep warm by being close to each other.)*

3. Why does Hannah think the filthy trough water tastes sweet? *(She is so thirsty that anything wet tastes wonderful.)*

4. Compare how Hannah feels when the train stops the second time but the doors do not open to the first time when she is given a drink. *(Answers will vary.)*

5. Why does Hannah's tongue feel as big as a sausage? *(Her mouth is dry from having no water.)*

6. What do you think will happen when Hannah arrives at the barracks? *(Answers will vary.)*

7. Compare how the rabbi feels about the situation and how the *badchan* feels about the situation in which they are thrown. *(The rabbi thinks that they "are in God's hands." The* badchan *believes that "This is the Devil's work, not God's.")*

8. What causes Fayge to fall and roll down the hill? *(Fayge tries to sidestep so as not to bump into Hannah when she fell.)*

9. What else can Shmuel do to help his bride-to-be? *(Answers will vary.)*

10. How does Gitl respond to Fayge's remark that they should run? *(Fayge says, "Run." Gitl replies, "There is nowhere to run, Fayge. We are where we are. Hush.")*

11. What causes Hannah to respond with vehemence to the woman in the blue dress? *(The three-fingered woman demands the blue ribbons from Hannah's hair.)*

12. How do you think Hannah feels as she is made to undress in front of all the others? *(Answers will vary.)*

13. What does Hannah think will happen as the women go into the showers? *(She thinks they will be gassed to death.)*

14. Do you agree with Gitl that they must live moment by moment? *(Answers will vary.)*

15. Why does Hannah feel regret after learning that Rachel died in the boxcar? *(She is sorry that she did not tell Rachel that she was her best friend.)*

16. How do you think Hannah and the others feel as they wait in the cold room after taking a shower? *(Answers will vary.)*

17. Why can't Hannah recall anything from the past after she gets her hair shaved? *(Answers will vary.)*

18. How is the gray dress Hannah chooses different from the blue sailor dress that Gitl loaned her? *(The gray dress is stained and torn; it is a true rag.)*

19. How does Hannah's experience with the man using the metal instrument make another hazy memory come to her mind? *(Answers will vary.)*

20. Why does the man with the tattooing pen urge Hannah not to forget the number on her arm? *(He tells her that if she forgets then life is indeed gone.)*

21. How would you describe the beds that Hannah and the others sleep in at night? *(They are small shelves without pillows or blankets.)*

22. Do you think that the soldier cared if the children got any food to eat? *(Answers will vary.)*

23. What did the soldier mean about going up the stack? *(He meant that Hannah would be killed and then burned in the oven with the smoke going up the smokestack.)*

24. Why does Gitl think they will be fed? *(because the soldier said that they are to learn to eat when food is given to you)*

25. Why do you think Hannah does not mind the rough surface of her bed? *(Answers will vary.)*

Supplementary Activities

1. Discussion/Writing: Have the class discuss the treatment of the Jews and reasons why these actions violated humanity. The students should then write a poem expressing their feelings.

2. Research: Have the students research the names of the Polish and German concentration camps during the war. They are to write a composition on the camps. Have them share the information with the class.

3. Critical Thinking: Have the students explain in their own words why they think Gitl told Hannah to "live moment by moment."

Chapters 13-14

Vocabulary

bellowing (105)	fuzzed (106)	clenched (106)	hovered (106)
muster (107)	unwarranted (107)	slab (108)	arbitrary (108)
orchestrated (108)	elusive (109)	preamble (109)	raucous (110)
mesmerized (110)	wooden clogs (115)	valises (115)	rattled (116)
starkly (118)	frostbite (118)	ramblings (120)	punctuating (121)

Discussion Questions

1. Why does Hannah crack her head on the shelf above her? *(She is startled by a strange bellowing sound.)*

2. Why do you think Hannah remembers the taste of the Seder food now when she hears the command of the soldier to hurry up and get in line? *(Answers will vary.)*

3. Gitl seems to be terribly upset as she gazes upon little Tzipporah. Why does she tell Hannah not to touch the child? *(Answers will vary.)* Do you think Gitl is being cruel to Hannah? Why or why not? *(Answers will vary.)*

4. How does Hannah react when she finally realizes that Tzipporah is dead? *(She tries to comfort Gitl.)*

5. Do you believe that Gitl had the right to slap Hannah when she tried to touch the dead child? *(Answers will vary.)*

6. Rivka tells Hannah to memorize her bowl. Why do you think the bowl is so important? *(The bowl is used for food, drinking, and washing.)* Do you own something that is as important to your survival as the metal bowl is to Hannah? *(Answers will vary.)*

7. Compare the food that Hannah is given to the food you ate today. Hannah eats her food before she realizes it is gone. Do you think she has enough to eat? *(Answers will vary.)*

8. What are the mixed feelings Hannah experiences as the three-fingered woman slaps Shifre? *(Hannah feels both guilty because she is the cause of Shifre being slapped and relieved the she did not get slapped.)*

9. Why do you think Hannah felt as if the officer's eyes were looking deep inside her? *(Answers will vary.)* Have you known someone that affected you in the same way? Describe this person and tell how he/she is related to you.

10. What kind of person do you think the three-fingered woman is? Does she seem to enjoy her job? *(Answers will vary.)*

11. What do you think would happen if all the prisoners began to run away? *(Answers will vary.)*

12. What do you think Rivka means when she tells Hannah, "If you are alive this minute, it is enough"? *(Answers will vary.)*

13. Rivka says, "As long as we can remember, all those gone before us are alive inside us." What does she mean by this? *(Answers will vary.)* Are there relatives or friends who have died that you can remember? Does your mother or father talk about relatives that they knew but have since died? Describe one of these relatives.

14. What gives Rivka the authority to tell Hannah and her friends how to stay alive at the camp? *(Rivka has survived a year at the camp.)* Why are the numbers on Rivka's arm so important to her? *(The numbers remind her of all the things that have happened to her and the things she has learned in camp.)*

15. Why does Hannah believe that God is not with them in the camp? *(Answers will vary.)*

16. How does Rivka answer Hannah's statement about God not being in the camp, but that it is the Devil's place? *(Rivka tells Hannah that God made the Devil, therefore God is in the camp.)*

17. Why do you think Rivka shares the rules of the camp with Hannah and Shifre? *(Answers will vary.)*

18. What rule do you think is the most important for the girls to follow in order to stay alive in the camp? *(Answers will vary.)*

19. Do you agree that Rivka, who is very young, can organize things in order for them to stay alive? *(Answers will vary.)*

20. Why is the garbage dump, or midden, so important to the young children? *(Commandant Breuer does not allow children under fourteen to be in the camp, therefore, the children run and hide in the garbage heap when he comes to inspect the prisoners.)*

21. How does Hannah feel about hiding in the garbage heap? How is her mind changed? *(She thinks it is disgusting; Rivka tells her, "Garbage can be Paradise" when it saves someone's life.)*

22. How does Rivka convince the girls to be grateful for the scuffed and worn shoes? *(Rivka tells them of her own experience with wooden clogs that her mother had carved for her.)*

23. How do you think Hannah and Shifre feel to have found a friend such as Rivka? *(Answers will vary.)*

24. What kind of person is Rivka? *(Answers will vary.)*

25. Why can't Hannah remember her family back in New Rochelle? *(Answers will vary.)*

Supplementary Activities

1. Creative Thinking/Poetry: Have the students create a Number such as Rivka's to tell about their life. Then have them write a six-stanza poem that relates the numbers to themselves. (Students should pattern their poems after Rivka's or Hannah's.)

2. Writing: Hannah manages to dodge a slap from the three-fingered woman but the slap hits Shifre. Hannah feels both guilty and relieved. The students should write about a time when the experienced both of these feelings. They may share with the class if they wish to do so.

3. Discussion: Hannah is embarrassed by the treatment she receives at the camp. Have the students talk about a time they were embarrassed. (Note: Instruct the students to focus on humorous embarrassing moments so students are not threatened by the discussion.)

4. Discussion: Rivka's faith seems to be a source of strength. Ask the students if they have a source (faith, family, friends, attitude) to help get them through difficult times.

Chapters 15-16

Vocabulary

cauldrons (122)	pervasive (123)	contorted (123)	splotchy (125)
luminous (126)	burnished (127)	cleft (127)	ominously (128)
cremated (128)	mounds (129)	harelip (133)	sonorous (134)
chaos (135)	eroded (135)	riveted (138)	spawning (139)
barreled (139)	relentlessly (139)	immeasurable (143)	endure (143)

Discussion Questions

1. How is the smell of the midden different from that of the camp? (*The smell of the midden is overwhelming, much worse than that of the smokestack and camp.*)

2. What does Hannah do as she takes the baby into the midden that upsets Leye? (*She leaves the baby's clothes on her.*)

3. Why do you think the commandant allows the children to stay in the camp? Do you agree with Hannah that it is all just some kind of awful game that is being played? (*Answers will vary.*)

4. Why does Hannah welcome the mindless sort of routine work in the camp? (*As long as she knows what to expect, she is not frightened.*)

5. How does Hannah get to work in the kitchen area? (*Rivka gave the* blokova *a gold ring as a bribe.*)

6. What do you think Rivka means as she tells Hannah that "a taker is not a giver and a giver is not a taker"? (*Answers will vary.*)

7. Why does Rivka admonish Hannah for giving her food to the child, Reuven, and then Rivka herself gives him half of her food? (*Answers will vary.*)

8. How does Hannah compare the Choosing of the Jews to the story of Hansel and Gretel? (*The witch checked Hansel's finger to see if he was fat enough for her to eat, just as the commandant is checking over the prisoners to see if they are strong enough to work. If not, they will be put into the oven just as the witch had planned to cook Hansel.*)

9. Why can't Hannah mention the words "corpse" or "death"? (*Rivka says that if the words are spoken then the event is recorded, and what is not recorded cannot be blamed. That is the way the soldiers want it and that is the way it will be.*)

10. Why is the commandant smiling as he comes back through the barracks? *(He has his page full of numbers which means he has completed the Choosing.)*

11. Why does Dr. Mengele pop into Hannah's head when she sees the smiling face of Commandant Breuer? *(She remembers a movie about the Angel of Auschwitz. Dr. Mengele was the commander who took great joy in putting the Jews to death.)*

12. Rivka is the great organizer of the camp. Who else organized a birthday scarf for Hannah? *(Gitl took the scarf.)* Do you think that it was right for Gitl to take the scarf without permission? *(Answers will vary.)*

13. Why do the women laugh when Gitl mentions the size of the commandant's boots? *(The size of his boots is a woman's size.)*

14. What news does Gitl relate? *(Gitl reveals that Fayge's father was Chosen along with many others from their village.)*

15. What does Gitl do and say to Hannah about her reaction to the death of the men? *(Gitl slaps Hannah on the cheek and tells her, "in here, we say the prayer for the dead properly, like good Jews.")*

16. Why does Gitl call each day that you are alive "one plus one plus one" the "Devil's arithmetic"? *(The rules are insane, but each day you are alive you are alive. Their world is in chaos, and they have no control over the evil that is happening, but any guidelines help.)*

17. Why does Hannah cry after she blurted out that her favorite food is pizza? *(Hannah is crying because she cannot remember what pizza is—only the word is stuck in her mind.)*

18. How did the *blokova* lose her fingers? *(She lost a finger each time she lost control of the prisoners and they rioted.)*

19. Why does Hannah feel a sudden coldness strike through her as the commandant's car rolls past the hospital where Reuven is standing with a bloody knee? *(She knows that the commandant will take him to Lilith's Cave to be gassed and then burned in the oven.)*

20. What change in the routine frightens the "long-termers" of the camp? *(The new arrivals do not go to the camps, but go directly to processing.)*

21. What story from her father does Fayge compare to the plight of the Jews? *(She compares the fight of Israel and the werewolf to that of the Jews and the German soldiers.)*

Supplementary Activities

1. Science/Health: Hannah and the other prisoners have only thin potato soup and crusts of brown bread to eat for each meal. The students can research the nutritional value of this food, and answer the following questions: Approximately how many calories did each person receive each day? What is the daily caloric requirement for an average ten-year-old girl?

2. Art: Have the students illustrate the scene at the water pump as Esther, Shifre, and Rivka listen to Hannah's stories from the future.

3. Compare/Contrast: Students can compare *The Devil's Arithmetic* to other things they have seen/read about the Holocaust, such as *Anne Frank: Diary of a Young Girl*.

Chapters 17-18

Vocabulary

proverb (145)	portents (146)	thudding (147)	bribed (147)
gagging (148)	staccato (148)	perimeter (148)	incredibly (148)
drawled (149)	muffling (149)	barbed wire (150)	defiantly (150)
undercurrent (152)	pocked (152)	volley (153)	parody (153)
scum (153)	irony (155)	superimposed (155)	babushka (158)

Discussion Questions

1. Why does Gitl tell Hannah that there is a plan? *(Gitl tells her because Hannah is her only flesh and blood.)*

2. Why do you think Gitl makes Hannah promise not to forget what is happening? *(Hannah is the only link to the past. She must remember what happened to her relatives.)*

3. Do you think Gitl is doing the right thing by not telling Hannah about the plan? *(Answers will vary.)*

4. Describe the days after Gitl tells Hannah that there is a plan. *(The days are routine, nothing seems to be happening: the death trains keep rolling toward the smokestack as the sky becomes red with the death smoke of the zugangi.)*

5. Does Hannah have any clue as to when the plan will come about? *(No, Hannah suspects nothing; there are no signs or portents.)*

6. How do you think Hannah feels as she realizes that the plan is finally coming true? *(Answers will vary.)*

7. Why isn't the barracks door locked? *(Gitl explains that some guards can be bribed to unlock the door.)*

8. What does Gitl mean when she says that Fayge has come to love her next bowl of soup more? *(Answers will vary.)*

9. Why does Hannah put both hands over her mouth as she feels the fear creeping over her? *(She is gagging herself so she won't scream out and reveal their position.)*

10. What is Hannah's fear as she and Gitl slip into the barracks door? *(She is afraid that they will be found out and then be Chosen.)*

11. What caused the *blokova* to awaken? *(Gitl and Hannah made noise as they hurried inside the barracks door.)*

12. How would you describe Gitl's excuse to the *blokova*? *(Answers will vary.)*

13. What kind of attitude does the *blokova* have toward the Jews? *(Answers will vary.)*

14. Why do you think Gitl crowded into the sleeping shelf with Hannah? *(Answers will vary.)* Why does Gitl laugh when she tells Hannah that the shoes Hannah dropped outside the barracks were not hers but the *blokova's*? *(Gitl knows that the shoes will be found and the* blokova *will be blamed.)*

15. What is Shmuel's attitude as he faces the commandant? *(Shmuel is defiant and brave.)*

16. Do you think the commandant is justified in being angry with the prisoners? *(Answers will vary.)*

17. According to the commandant, what is Berlin's "Final Solution to the Jewish Problem"? What does he mean? *(The solution is to process the Jews at once. All the Jews are to be killed.)*

18. Why do you think the commandant demands the other prisoners watch what happens to the six men? *(Answers will vary.)*

19. Why do you think Shmuel is searching with his eyes for Fayge? *(He loves her and wants to say his last good-bye.)*

20. What does Fayge mean as she cries to Shmuel, "The sky is our canopy. God's canopy. The sky"? *(Answers will vary.)*

21. Why do you think that the boy, Wolfe, showed no signs of sorrow or grief at the sight of the dead bodies? *(Answers will vary.)*

22. Yitzchak is not with the group that is captured and killed. What do you think happened to him? *(He probably escaped into the woods.)*

23. Compare nature around the camp to the horrific things that are happening inside the camp. Why is the contrast ironic? *(Answers will vary, but note that it is possible to have beauty surround you as death and suffering are present.)*

24. Why do you think Hannah feels compelled to tell her friends a story about the future? *(Answers will vary.)*

25. Do you think the young soldier enjoys choosing which girls will die? *(Answers will vary.)*

26. Why do you think Hannah takes Rivka's place to die? *(There must be one who can remember what is taking place. Hannah does not have a memory, but only a dream, therefore she lets Rivka stay to remember and tell what is happening to the Jews.)*

Supplementary Activities

1. Critical Thinking: When the *blokova* criticizes Jews for never doing anything quietly or efficiently, she is describing all Jewish people as having the same negative characteristics. This attitude is called "stereotyping." Ask students if they have encountered any common stereotypes in their lives. Pose the following questions for discussion: Why do some people stereotype others? How did the Nazis stereotype the Jewish people?

2. Brainstorm: Tolerance means treating people fairly, even though they are different from you. As a class, brainstorm ways that people with different beliefs or ideas can live together peacefully.

3. Pros/Cons: Discuss the pros and cons of escaping or attempting to escape from the concentration camp.

4. Music: Have the students select music that would express the mood of Chapter 18. The music could be played while the students are writing or reading.

Chapter 19, Epilogue, and What is true about this book

Vocabulary

expectantly (161)	draft (162)	prophet (162)	partisans (165)
liberated (165)	rations (165)	emigrated (165)	salvaging (166)
remnants (166)	Confirmation (167)	perusal (167)	malnutrition (168)
amalgam (168)	anonymous (168)	unimaginable (169)	indelible (169)
couched (169)	dehumanized (169)	galaxy (170)	

Discussion Questions

1. How do you think Hannah feels as she realizes that she is not at the death camp but back at her Grandpa's house with her family? *(Answers will vary.)*

2. Why is Hannah staring at the numbers on Aunt Eva's arm? *(She remembers that the number belongs to one of her friends at the camp.)*

3. Why hasn't Aunt Eva ever explained the numbers on her arm to Hannah? *(Hannah's mother hates for Aunt Eva to talk about it and Hannah never let her explain it.)*

4. Do you think Aunt Eva is surprised when Hannah begins to explain the numbers on Aunt Eva's arm? *(Yes, because she doesn't know how Hannah found the information.)*

5. What does Hannah realize as she is talking to Aunt Eva about the numbers? *(She realizes that Wolfe is Grandpa Will, Aunt Eva's brother.)*

6. How does Aunt Eva feel as she listens to Hannah say, "I remember. Oh, I remember"? *(Answers will vary.)*

7. Why does Aunt Eva tell Hannah about the end of the story when they are alone? *(She doesn't think that the rest of the family will believe Hannah was there at the camp.)*

8. Why does Gitl only weigh seventy-five pounds when she is liberated from the camp? *(She cares for the children of the camp and gives them part of her meager food rations.)*

9. Do you think Gitl and Yitzchak are happy when they emigrate to Israel? *(Answers will vary.)*

10. Is CHAYA a good name for the adoption agency that was founded by Gitl? Why or why not? *(Answers will vary.)*

11. Why do you think some people deny that the death camps ever existed, even though there is countless evidence that these horrible camps were real? *(Answers will vary.)*

12. What is your reaction to the misery and torture experienced in the camps? *(Answers will vary.)*

13. Do you think the world still remembers the six million Jewish people who were killed in the camps? Why or why not? *(Answers will vary.)*

14. Why do you think Jane Yolen wrote this book? *(Answers will vary.)*

Supplementary Activities

1. Speaking/Listening: Have students interview an older family member and ask that person to relate an important family story. Have the students retell the anecdote to their classmates.

2. Drama: Have the students reenact the scene where Hannah realizes she is back in New Rochelle.

Post-reading Discussion Questions

1. How might things have been different if Rivka had not been Hannah's friend?

2. What important lessons did Hannah learn from her experience?

3. Develop a graphic organizer on prejudice. (See page 34 of this guide.)

4. Do you think *The Devil's Arithmetic* is a good title for this book? Why or why not? Make up a new title for the story. Why would this be a good title for the book?

5. Have you read a story or seen a movie similar to this one? What is it? How is it similar? How is it different?

6. If you could change one part of this story, what would it be? Why?

7. If you had been part of Hannah's family in the past, would you have wanted to try to escape from the camp, even though you might be captured and killed?

8. How would the story have been different if it had been told by Rivka? by Shmuel? by the three-fingered woman?

9. Foreshadowing is the literary technique of giving clues about future events in a story. Where does the author use foreshadowing in *The Devil's Arithmetic?* What clues are given? What future events are being suggested?

10. What is bravery? Brainstorm. Use specific examples from the novel to support your ideas, or use examples of bravery you have witnessed in your life.

Post-reading Extension Activities

1. Write a short composition on how this story can help you make good decisions in your own life.

2. Imagine that you are one of the main characters and write a diary account of the events of a particular day in the story.

3. Make a collage of feelings evoked by the novel.

4. If you were to meet Jane Yolen, the author of *The Devil's Arithmetic,* what questions would you ask her?

5. Use a shoebox to make a diorama depicting your favorite scene from the book.

6. Design a different book jacket or poster to advertise the book.

7. Create a dictionary of Yiddish terms used in the book. Share it with the class.

8. Create a mobile to depict a scene from the book.

9. If you could illustrate three scenes from the story, which scenes would you choose? Why? Illustrate one of the scenes and display your drawing in the classroom.

10. Choose a part of the story that you liked very much. Find music that expresses the feeling of the story at that point. Record that section of the story on a tape along with the background music. Add the tape to the classroom listening library.

11. How do the main characters in *The Devil's Arithmetic* change as the story progresses? Why do the characters change? What events contribute to these changes? Choose one character from the book and complete a character chart (see pages 8-9 in this guide) that shows how the character reacts to events in the story and how those events change the character.

12. Write a diamente poem that describes one of the characters.

Example:

_____

Noun that describes the character

_____   _____   _____

Verbs that describe actions of the character

_____   _____   _____   _____

Adjectives that describe the character

_____   _____   _____

Verbs that describe actions of the character

_____

Noun that describes the character

Attribute Web

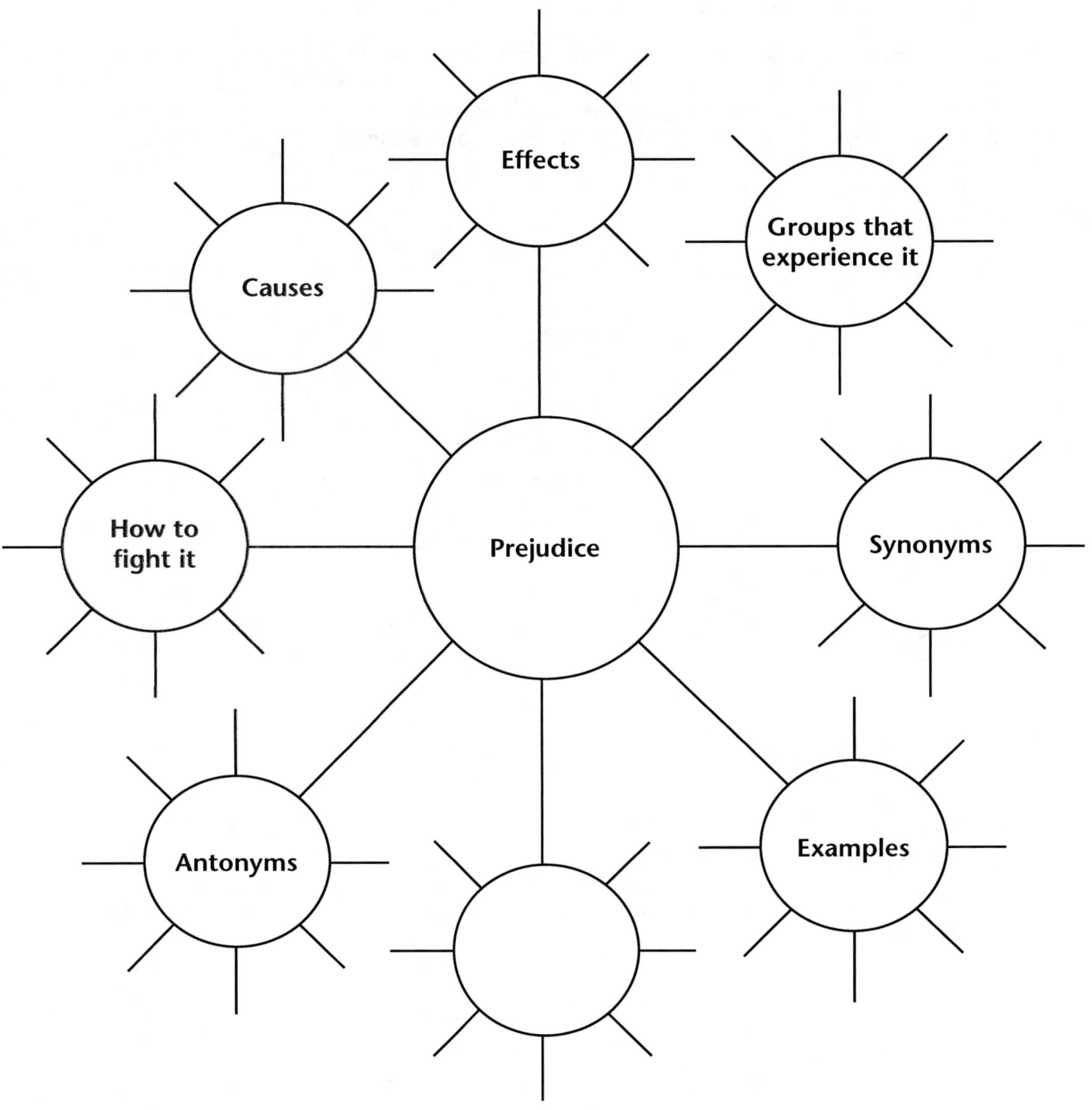

Assessment for *The Devil's Arithmetic*

Assessment is an ongoing process. The following ten items can be completed during the novel study. Once finished, the student and teacher will check the work. Points may be added to indicate the level of understanding.

Name _____ Date _____

Student   **Teacher**

_____   _____   1. Write a conversation that Hannah might have with Aunt Eva about the events that occurred after Chaya went into Lilith's Cave.

_____   _____   2. Name one conflict that happened to Hannah. How did this event change the way she viewed life?

_____   _____   3. Would you like to have Hannah as a friend? Why or why not?

_____   _____   4. Find five adjectives and five adverbs in the story that helped create the mood of the story. Use at least three of the adjectives and three of the adverbs in sentences.

_____   _____   5. Shoot a video advertisement to encourage another student to read this book. Show your advertisement to the class.

_____   _____   6. Rank the main characters in order from best liked to least liked. Write a paragraph explaining your ranking.

_____   _____   7. Make a character collage. Cut out words and pictures from magazines that describe one character in the novel. Put the character's name in the collage.

_____   _____   8. List at least three tragic scenes from the novel. Which characters were involved in each? Why do you consider the scenes tragic?

_____   _____   9. Write a letter to the author of *The Devil's Arithmetic* and tell her how you enjoyed the book.

_____   _____   10. Rewrite the ending of the story in the way you would have liked it to end.

Notes